A T

of the Poe ... ment

Pathways to Ecological Citizenship

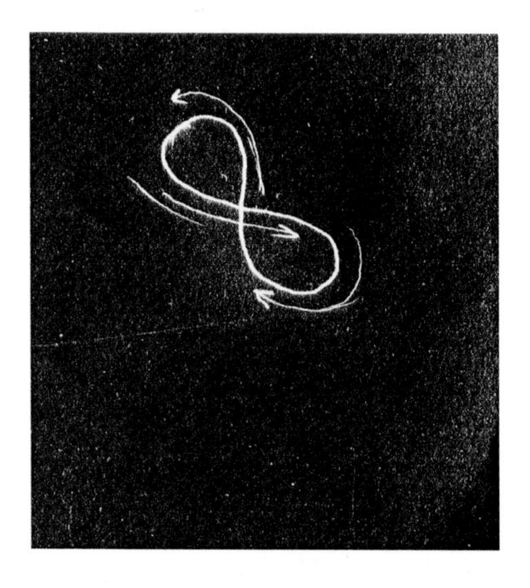

Shelley Sacks and Wolfgang Zumdick

Temple Lodge Publishing

2013

This is an atlas of the poetic continent

The places of the poetic continent are not physical places. They map the internal regions and contours of the inner human being that lives in a cosmos of other beings and life forms. They constellate the places of the soul.

The maps for this poetic continent – unspoken, unwritten, discovered only in each moment of engaging with the world – *are inspired by the constellations of the soul.* Such constellations offer distilled understandings on the path to a new society: a viable future of humane and ecological citizens – if we become aware of our nature as creative 'freedom-beings' and of the responsibility that is integral to this freedom.

The field of social sculpture illumines the importance of the encounter with oneself for one's encounter with the world and vice versa. Going out to come in, and coming in to go out: connecting inner shaping and outer action. As we glean understandings from these constellations they expand our capacities for being in the world and inform our practice in the field of social sculpture.

This ATLAS grew out of a social sculpture process in a city in 2009 that invited its citizens – individually and with each other – to enter a process of reflection on the question: *What am I doing in the world?* Since then we have realised that all our social sculpture explorations relate to the constellations of the poetic continent in as much as they offer insights for *coming to our senses.* For active citizenship, for eco-citizenship. For better inhabiting and shaping a more connective way of being in the world. For conscious 'interbeing'.

– *Shelley Sacks and Wolfgang Zumdick, Oxford 2013*

The Poetic Continent

We live on a planet with many continents, continents that we inhabit in countless different ways. But there is another continent not visible to the naked eye. An often unrecognised continent: the poetic continent.

It is a special continent since it lies both within us and without. And because it only comes alive *in* us, it is often overlooked and unseen. This means we cannot encounter it unless we develop the appropriate instruments for this meeting.

So what is this continent and what is its meaning for the events and struggles on the continents of daily life?

At every moment of our daily lives, we come into contact with things and situations, occasionally even with the contents of our own consciousness. We can be more or less aware of all these forms – whether they are an animal, plant, person, memory or social system. However, unless we enter them in the poetic mode they remain information summed up by concepts, on the one hand, and undisclosed forms from an unknown world, on the other.

Surprisingly, coming closer to the unknown is helped by not naming, by allowing whatever we encounter to disclose itself in us, in a mode without predetermined language. This is what happens when we enter the other with all eyes, all ears. In the artistic mode.

If we really encounter things in this way, we are entering a world that is open. But in this openness is also the challenge: to come to know without foreclosing.

A child is playing in the room. I can see it there, and can see it is playing. All my senses are involved. It would be the same if I encountered an elephant. In both situations there are many things and elements to see, observe, take note of. The soft curls of the child's hair. Its fingers exploring the contrast of the floor's surface to the sticky juice it has spilled on the floor. The infinitely delicate touch of the elephant's 'fingers' on the end of its trunk, and the gentle way it touches the earth with its big heavy foot. Through these and myriad other details we come to experience the child and the elephant: as undivided and indivisible realities.

These realities can only be experienced and come to life in us if we do not too quickly distance ourselves from them with conceptual language or prejudiced attitudes, desires and values. If we do not experience the child or the elephant and only gather information, particularly via a screen, we may well come to the concept 'child' or 'elephant', and have information about what they were doing, whilst nevertheless having bypassed the reality of the child *and* the elephant. Having bypassed their unfathomable mystery.

This kind of openness also engenders and enables respect. And it is this respect that further opens the doors to the secrets of the other and enables the hidden side, the poetic dimension, to be revealed. *This coming closer to the other is also a coming closer to oneself.*

By opening our ears and eyes, by opening all our senses, the self enters the world. The deeper and more profound the encounters with the world, the clearer and deeper are the imprints remaining in one's mind. This self, nourished by the depth of the impressions we have in our daily life, is therefore the inner space of our outer experience.

But what is this inner space, this inner chamber we call mind? Is it simply a warehouse, where memories are taken out of storage now and then … where we shake off the dust of time past, getting cold or warm feelings as we re-think what has happened, what we felt and thought, as we recall our wishes and longings? The more we look into what occurs we recognize that the contrary is the case. Memories are not dead, static images. We can re-enter, rediscover and re-live them. And even if they sometimes have a life of their own, it is nevertheless possible to work with them, deepen them, and reconsider them.

But this inner chamber also enables us to live in the present. Whatever confronts us, whatever we meet in the world has to be registered in ourselves. This can be done rationally, as we do with information, or it can be lived.

What does this mean – to live the events and occurrences of the outer world? Is it a kind of 'participation mystique', an experience where all difference is dissolved through inhabiting so deeply that we are indistinguishable from the thing perceived? Yes, this is one way of coming closer to the world. This mystic union, that the ancient Greeks describe as *hen kai pan*, where one is united with everything, united with the One.

There is however another way of coming close to all that is outside and within us. It appears quite similar to 'participation mystique' as it also involves a complete immersion in and inhabiting of the thing perceived. But this inhabiting coexists with an inner awareness that involves *seeing what one sees*, and *hearing what one hears* – without losing the *being-one-with*.

It means entering and embracing the world, being astounded by its creatures, events and occurrences in myself, like a child. Full of wonder. I wander through its forms and processes, like the pathways of a forest. Immersed in its objects, forms and events, but also seeing what I see, the unknown unfolds within and around me. At the same time, I acquire a special kind of *connective distance* ... a special position in which I am immersed but remain conscious.

This is the space of insights. Here I can see connections. Get new perspectives. Link current impressions with earlier experiences and understandings. I not only *come to my senses* in the present but I can *make sense*. This is the realm of relatedness. Of being in touch with what is and the choices I can make, must make. The poetic continent can therefore also be understood as a synonym for all those attempts that reconnect our souls to the sources of life: through active seeing, listening and experiencing with all our twelve senses. Entering the poetic continent in this sense is about the meeting of worlds. Human beings seem to need this experience as flowers need water. Our inner worlds are so depleted that they urgently have to be nourished and educated anew.

Poeisis means to be in things. And so, the poetic continent truly comes alive when I am fully present, not only to the beauty of things, to this awesome world, but also to the questions, and the mess: to the challenges for shaping a different kind of world, and to my potential for making choices. This is also part of the poetic continent. My freedom and my response-ability.

Our inner space is the workspace. A permanent rent-free space available to all; an arena hosted by our inner capacities that we could describe as imagination, inspiration and intuition. The thoughts and insights that arise in this workspace are active and show us that the poetic continent is manifest in us.

The poetic continent is therefore the 'u-topos' that exists and comes to life in every genuine encounter.

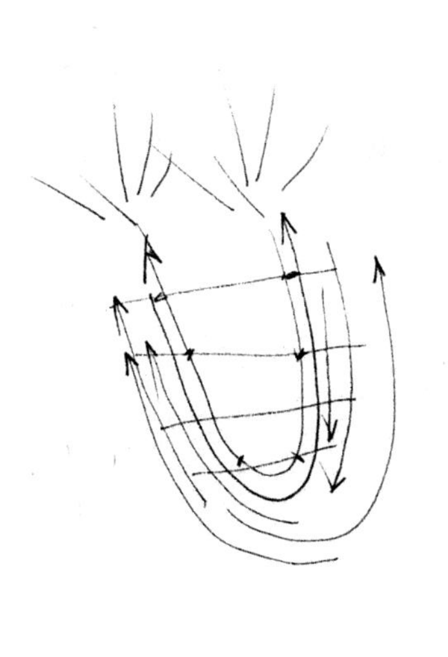

The Territory

Welcome to the field of transformation
to the territory
in which insights and questions
are forces
forces that move in us
and in the world
that enhance
our ability to see anew,
and contribute
to the future's unfolding.

An invisible plastic process
in us
and in the world
no less real than wood or steel
than facts –
a sphere
in which questions are forces
that guide us
open up new directions
allow answers to emerge

A territory
in which values, insights,
understandings are materials

A region in which we meet ourselves
and stand naked before the question

What am I doing in the world?

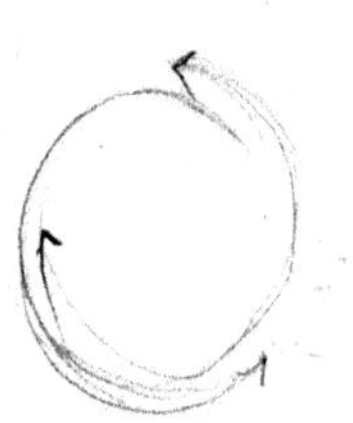

I – you

What does it mean, to meet oneself?

Is there in us this other, that I am, and yet am not?
Who are we, are we less or are we more?
What does it mean to be here, in this place?

What does one see when one looks in a mirror?
The eyes alone?
Hands?
Arms?
Mouth?
Is this the place where we encounter?

And beneath this sheath of skin?

Is it not my heart that beats,
my mouth that laughs,
my eyes that look into yours?

And what might come to pass
if we meet,
and briefly touch?

Is it not I who, in the loved one,
meets one's self?
Is it not the self that first encounters
in itself, the other?

The Constellations

22. Dec. 2007

The Land of Questions

A question is a light
that beckons me in my unknowing,
and illumines answers that hide

A question is a boat
that carries me into new territory
and stops me from sinking back into the known

A question is the fecund shadow
that moves us beyond what we habitually assume,
beyond what seems to be fixed,
beyond the inherited answers of systems
that unless we realise it,
forcibly shape our lives.

As children, profound questions
weave through our days,
but soon we are led to believe
that they are answered
by what we learn.

So, a question is a gift and danger.

It is not silenced by all the information and ways of seeing we are socialised into. It initiates movement amongst the fixed forms.

And so the need to open up spaces, in our private and public lives, to (re)discover and follow our questions, to take them as companions and guides, so we can work with them to re-view and re-shape both personal and social forms.

11 Jan 2008

The Land of Questions

No physical force is restraining us from devoting our courage and creativity to the protection of life on Earth. What then is stifling our responses as individuals and as a society?
– *Joanna Macy*

In the dark light of our success we turn on the fluorescents
They give an even brightness and cast no shadows

With what sense organs can we perceive this complex horror?
With what sense organs can I perceive the world's suffering?
With what sense organs can I perceive the future's answers?

Yes/No? Yes/No?
Which way to go?

Welcome to the place of questions and a Landing Strip for Souls
– *Shelley Sacks*

I beg you, to have patience with everything unresolved in your heart and to try to love the questions themselves as if they were locked rooms or books written in a very foreign language. Don't search for the answers, which could not be given to you now, because you would not be able to live them. And the point is to live everything. Live the questions now. Perhaps then, someday far in the future, you will gradually, without even noticing it, live your way into the answer.
– *Rainer Maria Rilke*

My Land

The Land of Fear

Fear paralyzes. It makes us passive.
Actions infused with fear are not free, because they cannot confront the cause of the fear without fear. We stand naked and yet cloaked in fear.

Then again, fear can also mobilise us internally.

If we refuse to be intimidated, and face the problem, we may experience that we are stronger than the fear and that which causes it; that internally we are stronger than any external threat.

Paul Celan describes another aspect of fear. According to him, 'we need to go through art into the narrowest constrictions' of our being, and by this he means inner constrictions: the apprehensions, anxieties, desperations, the fear of one's own pain as well as that of others. His experience as a poet shows him that art is able to illuminate the threats hidden within, and deal with them in an active and imaginal way. Experiencing the threat as an image that we ourselves produce is of great significance for the soul.

Much is achieved if we can see our own fear. Dealing with it in an active way can mobilise our powers of transformation and of healing.

The courage to face what frightens us and to examine the situation we fear can shift the often distorted and limited image that causes our fear. And so we can be changed. Through working with our fear in this way we gain both a certain freedom as well as understanding the nature of the fear.

Furcht ↑↓

The Land of Fear

Every crisis is a possibility.
– *I Ching*

Apatheia is a Greek word that means non-suffering. Given its etymology, 'apathy' is the inability or refusal to experience pain.

The problem [...] lies not with our pain for the world, but in our repression of it. Our efforts to dodge or dull it surrender us to futility, or, in systems terms, cut the feedback loop and block effective response.
– *Joanna Macy*

no longer fearing my shore
you enter my door
uncover your wounds
and offer your river to me
so I can swim into your words
– *Shelley Sacks*

We must look for danger from within, not fear the danger from without. The first corrodes the soul, the second polishes it. ... No outside power can really degrade a human being. One can only degrade oneself.
– *Gandhi*

Life will never be without fear. There are countless things that cause fear. Life is interwoven with suffering. But if we push it away it will engulf us more and more. Similarly if we ignore the unnecessary suffering that surrounds us – the human coldness, cruelty, aggression – it will never go away. To look into the world of fears and all that frightens us, enables us to find new answers and other ways of being in the world.
– *Wolfgang Zumdick*

My Land

The Land of Challenge

The German word for challenge *Herausforderung* is close to the English word *provocation*. Just like pro-vocation, it has two parts: 'heraus' and 'forderung', which mean 'coming out' and 'call' or 'demand'. It is *the call to come out* ... out of old habits, out of a self-involved mode of being, out of the habits that diminish our self through lack of encounter. Coming out of our self in this way means to inhabit the other without judgement and explore this region of the poetic continent.

Once out of our cocoon, we are confronted with a host of questions. How shall we live with each other? How shall we live in the world? These questions have to do with acknowledging our being *in* the world, with others, and shaping a viable future.

Turning our familiar view of the future on its head, Beuys declares: 'The cause lies in the future'. Now, it is not the past that determines the future, but rather what can be expected of it. And so, the future is what we make of it, in the here and now. We enact the future in every moment! The question 'How do we want to live?' has therefore to be entered with clarity and awareness.

But everything cannot be planned. We are on a journey of uncertainties. And yet, the conditions that we shape can be different. They can ensure every being their rights, including every human being their dignity: a livelihood, shelter and a way of finding themselves in the world.

This is the greatest challenge we are confronted with: the future that longs for us!

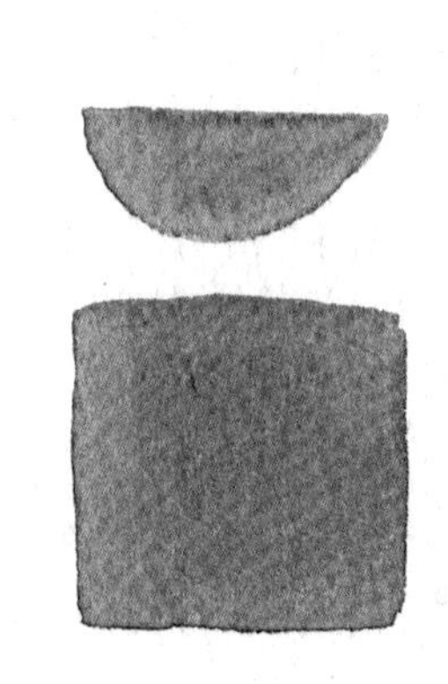

The Land of Challenge

...What happens to our own and other species, to the legacy of our ancestors, to our unborn generations, and to the living body of the Earth? The source (of such questions) lies less in concerns for the personal than in comprehensions of collective suffering. ...this is akin to the original meaning of compassion: 'suffering with'. It is the distress we feel on behalf of the larger whole of which we are a part. It is the pain of the world itself experienced in each of us.

– Joanna Macy

The human being is able, from a position of freedom, to shape and work on his life just as he can shape and work on material.

– Karl Jaspers

When we least expect it life sets us a challenge to test our courage and willingness to change. At such a moment, there is no point in pretending that nothing has happened or in saying that we are not yet ready. The challenge will not wait. Life does not look back. A week is more than enough time for us to decide whether or not to accept our destiny.

– Paulo Coelho

A deep understanding of our individual and collective responsibility to humanity as a whole, and to the environment, is essential to our survival in the globally interdependent world of the 21st century, let alone to human flourishing. Children and youth are among the most vulnerable to the effects of poverty, war, and other problems, and the least directly represented in policy-making; yet they are key to long-term solutions. What are the qualities that future citizens will need to respond to these challenges with compassion, wisdom, creativity, and skill?

– Dalai Lama, 2009

My Land

The Land of Confidence

How does confidence come about? It comes from experience.

If confidence were not connected to experience, it would be hope. Hope is devoid of the substance of experience, which makes confidence such a source of power. Confidence draws its strength from the experience that we are able to solve problems and to deal with seemingly dead-end situations.

So, only if we experience that negative things can be transformed and not simply kept at bay, can we be truly confident. If problems arise, we can, with such awareness, be confident of our ability to solve them.

Without confidence one hesitates before one's problems. One does not confront them. And the danger is that we then end up accepting what is damaging. Accepting too much damage leads to a sense of hopelessness.

This is why too few people have the liberating experience that each one of us has the potential to change: to create more satisfying life forms; to develop new ways of reacting to challenges from both within and without.

This is why we need places where confidence is nurtured and the potential to change can be experienced and lived. Places where we get a sense of what it means to move internally; where we can picture the problems and use our imaginative space to explore alternatives. Alternative pictures are an inner experience of how things could be different. They enable the initial shift of consciousness that is needed for further change.

Zuversicht (Antwort)

The Land of Confidence

S: Leibniz was convinced about the overarching harmony of the universe. He speaks of a universal harmony. In fact, if we envision the coherence of things in the world: of thinking and being, of air, water, fire and earth, of animals and plants, of the elements iron, hydrogen, chlorine and sodium, of the circling stars, over millions of years, of the conditions that allow for evolution, and that there are such things as mathematics, time and space that are calculable; of the sun, that gives us warmth and light ... an infinite number of factors that interweave and fit together ... if one fully enters this image one will perceive an a unique and wonderful harmony.

Z: Why then are we so obstinate, refusing to listen to the great laws of creation?

Perhaps this desire for freedom, which does not shy away from failure, despair and death, which obstinately wants to know to the point of self destruction, denying everything, questioning everything, is at the same time also one of the greatest gifts humans have? Perhaps it is precisely from this perspective, from a profound experience of failure, that we are able to grasp the basic idea of beauty at all. If beauty is no longer simply given, we might be able to recognise that we have the freedom to create it ourselves. That we have the capacity to shape the forms and conditions of our lives like a Bach fugue.

So, the question is ... how do I, as an individual, come out of my shell and learn to better understand myself, the world and my fellow human beings? And how can we together develop forms and ways that may not be the best possible, but that certainly begin to come closer to this?

– Extract from a talk about Leibniz between Gerhard Stamer and Wolfgang Zumdick

My Land

The Land of Wonder

The biggest wonder is that something exists, and not nothing.

Existence can only really be valued if we view the world from the perspective of non-existence: nothing is unimportant, nothing is more important, nothing is worthless.

Once we are able to live into the complexity of the world from a perspective of wonder, it will exhibit new, yet unseen, hidden aspects. Simplicity, wonder and questioning are not only the source of knowledge, they are also its goal.

Unless we come to the heart of all things with the eyes of wonder, we cannot recognise their distortedness, live their agony, or hear their suffering. Seeing the wonder in the world is therefore not the contrary of the political, the social and of working for change. It is the only way that the discrepancy between a living river and a poisoned river can be experienced in my own body; between what could be and what has gone wrong. Awe mobilises me internally. Wonder lets me experience the gaps between what it is and what is needed. Through wonder I hear the voice of the world.

Seeing the political and social dimension with the senses of wonder, it is no longer dry. It is a field of unimaginable beauty and appropriateness: forms of distribution, of cooperation, of agriculture; forms of schooling that enable the human being to flourish and make better decisions about how to live in this world. Social forms derived from entering the world with the eyes of wonder could be called *aesthetic organisation* or *social sculpture*! And so our task: embodying insights derived from the wondrous world in humane and ecologically sensitive forms.

27 Dec. 2007

The Land of Wonder

Among all beings, only the human being, prompted by the voice of existence, the wonder of all wonders, recognises that being is.
  – *Martin Heidegger*

The mystical is not how the world is, but that it is.
  – *Ludwig Wittgenstein*

We all walk in mysteries. We are surrounded by an atmosphere about which we still know nothing at all.
  – *Johann Wolfgang von Goethe*

Imagine a limitless expanse of water: above and below, before and behind, right and left, everywhere there is water. In that water is placed a jar filled with water. There is water inside the jar and water outside, but the jar is still there. The 'I' is the jar.
  – *Ramakrishna*

Since music creates particular patterns in liquids and solids alike, it is no surprise that it can also profoundly influence human beings … music is an organising force.
  – *Paul Ashton*

But now   there is silence   and the words   make
help make   the silences   .

    I have nothing to say   and I am saying it
and that is poetry   as I need it   .

    This space of time   is organized
                                    We need not fear these   silences.

  – *John Cage*

My Land

The Land of Interiority

Intimacy, inwardness and interiority have much in common – embodied by the shared *in* at the beginning of each word.

But unlike the state of inwardness in which we are often closed-off to the outer world, to others, interiority has a spaciousness. It is a state of inner space.

In this inner space I have the mobility to move around and find a quiet vantage point. It is space from which to see, to receive: to *take in* what appears as outside of me. But it is also the space in which I can *see* myself see, *hear* myself hear, become aware of what I feel.

Although this perceptive, enlivened state can be opened up by intimacy, by my closeness to you or other beings, I still need the internal space, the interiority, to return to myself… to feel you, to really be near you, to appreciate and value you, to respect you and to see what you need.

It is this gift of interiority that makes love possible, freedom possible, and the conscious shaping of our lives.

This interior space that James Hillman calls the 'theatre of memory' is a 'rent free workspace' available to us all. Into this space where we take in the forms of the outer world, where we look at our views, values and positions, we are also able to see the lenses with which we view and experience the world. This helps us move beyond the passivity and helplessness that comes from thinking that we are in a world not of our making. When we recognize that we can alter the lenses with which we see and shape the world, we recognise something of our freedom and of our choices. We can then become enlivened participants, whose capacities for appropriate action are greatly enhanced!

The Land of Interiority

I gradually became aware that my interiority was inseparable from my exteriority, that the geography of my city was the geography of my soul.

– *Aleksandar Hemon*

I took great care to understand every single image … and above all, to realise them in actual life. That is what we usually neglect to do. We allow images to rise up, and maybe we wonder about them, but that is all. We do not take the trouble to … draw ethical conclusions … It is equally a grave mistake to think that it is enough to gain some understanding of the images … Insight into them must be converted into ethical obligation … The images place a great responsibility upon a human being.

– *C. G. Jung*

[Like two sides of one coin …] the Physical and the Psychic, the Without and the Within, Matter and Consciousness, are all found to be functionally linked in one tangible process.

– *Teilhard de Chardin*

I don't talk about consciousness, I talk about interiority.

– *Ken Wilber*

Our human capacity for deep interiority – the fact that we have a consciousness that has developed the capacity to reflect upon itself – is the very leading edge of the inner dimension of the evolving Kosmos.

– *Andrew Cohen*

… listen to the voice of the wind and the ceaseless message that forms itself out of silence

– *Rainer Maria Rilke*

My Land

The Land of Encountering Oneself

Who do I encounter when I encounter myself? Is I 'another' as the French poet, Arthur Rimbaud has written? Am I perhaps a stranger to myself? Someone I have still to encounter, to come closer to, and who only slowly opens to me?

Every encounter with oneself is also an encounter with a known stranger in me. A remembering as well as a discovery in a literal sense. Something very active: I re-member, I create and re-create internally (er-innere) a hidden part of my soul. I un-cover, remove layer upon layer of prejudice, illusion and opinion that conceals a clear perception of myself.

In encountering myself I also encounter the other.

Through this encounter the boundary to the other becomes more porous. They come closer to me and I to them.

However, to encounter myself also means to meet myself in *my relation* to the other. I am a relational being.

When I look carefully at these relations I see a picture of how I act and react in the world. And in this moment of looking at myself, I also unearth the hurtful parts of a relationship. By bringing them into the light the opportunity of reshaping and working with them exists.

The human being is a being in becoming and the encounter with oneself is a primary arena of change.

2 Jan 2008

The Land of Encountering Oneself

I am not I
I am this one
walking beside me whom I do not see,
whom at times I manage to visit,
and whom at other times I forget;
the one who remains silent while I talk,
the one who forgives, sweet,
when I hate,
the one who takes a walk
when I am indoors,
the one who will remain standing
when I die.

– *Juan Ramon Jimenez*
[Translation Robert Bly]

Most people begin ... to seek solutions for their own problems. Eventually, though, [they discover] that personal solutions must involve solutions to society's problems, and vice versa. The basis of this ... is the realization that every person is made up of all the elements that are not herself. All the other people in human society are within each one of us. All those who are victims of injustice, and perpetrators of injustice, are within each of us. So everyone shares responsibility for the social conditions that create every social evil. Each one of us, if we are fully aware, will identify with the criminal as well as the victim.

– *Thich Nhat Hahn*

Dignity comes into being through meeting: I come to know because the world connects me with myself.

– *Lothar Gryczan*

My Land

Land of Comprehending

The land of philosophy.

Can we ever hope to completely understand the world?

Does it, as many philosophers believe, shy away from all attempts to grasp it?

Or have we not yet developed the appropriate organs to be able to understand it?

Even Kant, the great sceptic on this question, recognised possibilities of experience other than those based on rational forms of knowledge.

When I see a tree, it is more than its trunk, its roots, its leaves, its branches. It is also more than the seed, which carries the tree within it, like its dream.

The tree is an image and a promise that awaits us.

Each idea, whether of a tree or nature's suffering, of a chair or the global economy – presents us with both a question and a challenge. On the one hand, all these things are very close to us. On the other they are also strange and unfamiliar. And so they challenge us to (re-)discover them through our inner activity for ourselves.

Everything that we encounter wants to be understood.
Everything that we encounter begs to be understood.

31 Dec 2007

The Land of Comprehending

We shall never fully understand ourselves, yet we can and will far surpass mere understanding.

– *Novalis*

What is most important lies in what is hidden, in what we do not understand … Because, given the sheer magnitude of what we humans actually have to understand, I understand nothing, and neither do you! Although: I do understand a little, and one day we will be able to understand it all. This is why we are starting now.

– *Joseph Beuys*

Every process in nature, rightly observed, awakens in us a new organ of perception.

– *Johann Wolfgang von Goethe*

If concepts alone had a value, then we would need no colours, no images, no drawings, no imagination, sculptures, sounds, music, dance, theatre, nothing at all! Everything would be able to be verbalized accurately by means of concepts. Concepts are structures that are also important. But if they exist in a one sided way, they are clearly the absolute death of culture … After six months, if not nourished by the imagination, which is to say, by gothic portals, by cathedrals, by the symphonies of Bach, Mozart, Beethoven, by the pictures of Rembrandt, and so on, concepts would be like corpses. Even the rational concepts of physics basically only come to life through imagination, because the imagination goes much deeper into the evolutionary root of things and delivers life, so to speak, to language.

– *Joseph Beuys*

My Land

Land of Democracy

Democracy means encounter.

In the democratic process we encounter the views, opinions, perspectives and ideas of others that we do not necessarily share. In this sense democracy is always a challenge to our thinking. It is a place of coming to consciousness.

How do we want to live? How do we want to improve the unsatisfactory forms? These are the kinds of questions that any community or group must attend to. A democratic process is therefore a place of enlivening questions!

But how do we organise and think together about these processes so that they are living and responsive? We know how to dance together, play football together, sleep together, sing together. What we don't yet seem to do very well is think together!

If our current ritualised forms of exploring questions are not satisfactory we need to create new forms. Beyond theoretical discourse. Exploring new forms of encounter, as individuals, on a shared planet, who need to develop common aims.

Such questions are not only about the structures and processes we need but about the capacity for listening, for empathy and for imagination. We have to enter this world as lovers to unleash the Eros that democracy so needs; the enlivened perception to help us discover forms of organisation that can save us and the planet; forms of organization that see the individual as the basis for new community, and community as the opportunity for the growth of the individual.

Land of Democracy

We need equal rights because we are different!
– Joseph Beuys

We need to … 'recognize the links between the environment, democracy and peace and bring them to worldwide attention' … we need 'to encourage community efforts to restore the earth at a time when we face the ecological crises of deforestation, desertification, water scarcity and a lack of biological diversity. … Unless we properly manage resources like forests, water, land, minerals and oil, we will not win the fight against poverty. And there will not be peace. Old conflicts will rage on and new resource wars will erupt unless we change the path we are on.'
– Wangari Maathai

The dignity of the human being is inviolable. To respect and protect it is the duty of all state authority.
– The German Constitution

Words, after speech, reach
Into the silence.
– T. S. Eliot

Earth Democracy generates a radical shift in our paradigms and in our patterns of production. It offers real solutions to resource exhaustion, peak oil, climate change, disposability of people, and the erosion of democracy.
– Vandana Shiva

The sacrament of the future is to encounter.
– Rudolf Steiner

My Land

The Land of Thinking

What is thinking? Something that happens only in our mind? The mere reflection of an external, factual reality?

We are here, the world is there, and it determines us without us really knowing how. Thinking is a force that makes the other, the external world, accessible to us bit by bit. It is something that makes the world in-and-for-itself into a world *for us*: the *inner* outside world as well as the familiar outside!

Thinking is a force that not only passively receives reality but also actively creates it. Our thoughts, our ideas, also shape our reality. Ideas that derive from hate, fanaticism, selfishness, envy, chauvinism and intolerance are a part of human history and of its present. But they don't have to haunt human history forever.

We need to find other ways of thinking that lead us in other directions. The reality we experience through thought is often understood as a pale, shadowy reflection of the real. But thinking is by no means bloodless and dreary. Thinking is a creative force. One could also call it an imaginative and creative force that is responsible for bringing us closer to our existence in the first place. Through thinking we inwardly live the world. If we don't digest the world in ourselves through thought, our experience of the world remains shadowlike, because the active 'I', our will, does not truly reach into the depths of the things encountered.

From this perspective, thinking means reworking the world in us, reforming it, reshaping it. Understood in this way, thinking is both a radical opportunity and a challenge. A true responsibility. How we think is how we see and live in the world. It is in our thinking that we must therefore also become artists of change!

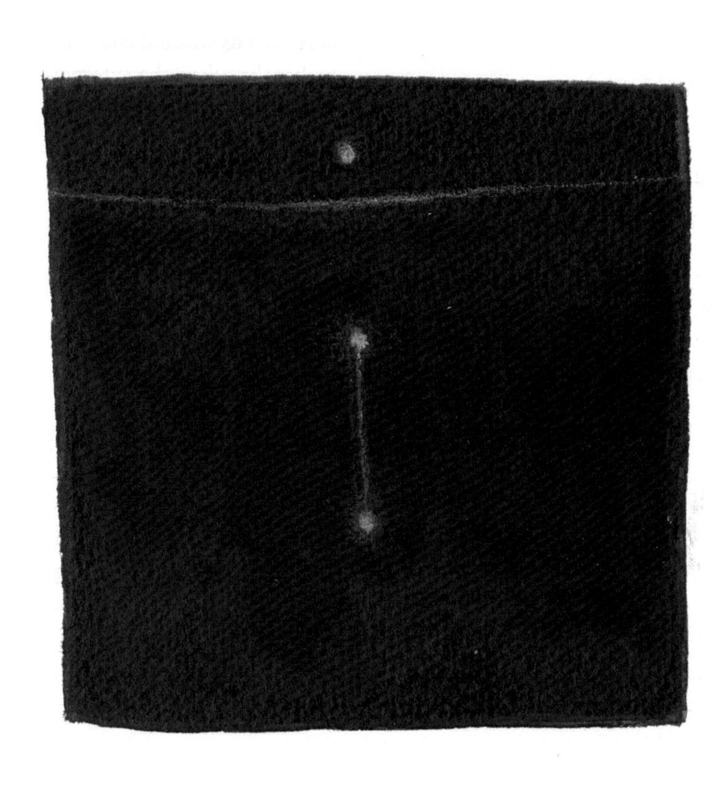

The Land of Thinking

The belief that the world has been formed by thought and is still constantly being formed this way, is what makes the practice of thinking meaningful in the first place.

– *Rudolf Steiner*

The forms in which thoughts manifest are unlimited and they shape the circumstances of life. Circumstances are therefore as unlimited as the different ways in which thought can take action [...] for the realms of life and death are created by thought, are attached to thought and governed by thought; thought is the master of every possible situation.

– *from a Mahayana scripture*

No matter how big the basic cosmological entity 'world' might be, no matter how many light-years and speeds of light are bandied about and whatever they may or may not be – human thought is even greater because it encompasses all this.

– *Joseph Beuys*

We have to get right down to the habit level to change things. And to do this we must become the seer that sees.

– *Nisreyasananda*

The more we regard ourselves as complex thought machines the less we are able to understand the nature of thought. Thinking is more than information and an input-output process. It is an imaginative act. We can only become free thinking agents of change if we engage in the world with imagination in order to rethink the conditions for the possibility of change.

– *Wolfgang Zumdick*

My Land

The Land of Attentiveness

The word attention contains the word 'attend'.

I attend when something unexpected happens, when something disrupts the routine.

In this sense, attention can be understood as something provoked from the outside: an event causes us to take note or look deeper, to become attentive to what is happening.

But there is also an attentiveness that we initiate ourselves.

This has to do with interest. *Inter-esse* which in Latin means 'to be present', 'presence', and 'to participate' is both *a taking part in* and a *being present*. Here and nowhere else. What Husserl and Heidegger describe as 'presencing'!

This kind of attentiveness involves going out to the other through taking part in the other. Whether through active listening, active seeing, or any other form of deep appreciation that observes and encounters but does not judge, interest in the other is the motivating force. It is the movement that takes me out of myself and into an erotic relationship with the other. And yet I do not lose myself in this going out. I am as attentive to myself as to you. I and the other are both equally present in the moment of presencing.

Attention as an erotic movement that moves out and embraces the other makes us lovers of the world.

The world is all its beauty and its pain longs for and needs this attentive embrace.

The Land of Attentiveness

'... the most important precept of all is to live in awareness, to know what is going on ... to be aware of what we do, what we are, each minute.' When we are totally mindful – in direct contact with reality, not just images of reality – we realize that 'all phenomena are interdependent ... endlessly interwoven. [This is] the principle of interbeing.'

– *Thich Nhat Hahn*

Mankind is in great danger, and the only solution is to become more conscious. The only real danger that exists is man himself.

– *Carl Jung*

The phrase 'gifting attention' – in German 'Aufmerksamkeit schenken' - is of primary significance in our attempt to connect with the world and to shape a viable future. Yes, attention is the first gift that we give to the world.

– *Shelley Sacks*

The faster life gets, the quicker our attention and perception has to act and react. In such accelerated times a certain depth of encounter is lost. This is not a pessimistic pronouncement, but a phenomenological observation. There is a kind of degeneration in our perception and the carefulness of being gets lost. Something that bothers one very much today can tomorrow get completely forgotten in the maelstrom of information and demands that confront one. This is the reason why we need to find ways to attend more deeply and create more careful listening processes. Only in this way can we 'slow down' sufficiently to be *actively* engaged and responsive in the world.

– *Wolfgang Zumdick*

My Land

The Land of Intuition

I am here. You are there. The difficulties, challenges and questions are there. The wondrous world is there. All outside me. If I approach this 'outside' with predetermined ideas or judgements it remains outside. I stand outside. This is the critical stance. It leaves me distant and alone. Bereft of intuition. Bereft of ways of knowing that enable me to act from any basis other than logic, assessment and calculation. But if I stay open, if I observe and perceive without judgement, if I encounter without scepticism and fear, what is outside enters me. I experience it in the only place I can: in me, in my mind's eye, my imagination, without the distancing barriers of judgement. Then whatever is 'outside' becomes alive in me. It begins to disclose itself in me. This engaged imagination is the first step to intuition.

As this disclosing takes place and the observed lives and moves in me, new insights begin to appear. Arise. Stream in. I am now the receiver of what I did not know. One could call this inspiration. If I stand in this stream and allow this new knowing to speak in me, I know what needs to be done. You and all outer events speak *in* me. I have come to understanding through another mode of knowing: through intuition.

Intuition is not then the 'other' of thought, but rather another kind of thought. Not rational, logical thought, but phenomenological thought that begins with imagination: with close noticing, with taking in the world through *all* my senses. Understood in this way we might also understand how intuition enlivens and mobilises us internally. And how we can therefore speak of *moral* intuition. Perhaps all intuition in this sense carries the insight of what needs to be done. It is then the personality or ego that accepts or turns away. That rejects or acts on the intuition.

The Land of Intuition

The intuitive mind is a sacred gift and the rational mind is a faithful servant. We have created a society that honours the servant and has forgotten the gift. We will not solve the problems of the world from the same level of thinking we were at when we created them. More than anything else, this new century demands new thinking. We must change our materially based analyses of the world around us to include broader, more multidimensional perspectives.

– *Albert Einstein*

Mysterious, even in broad daylight,
Nature won't let her veil be raised:
What your spirit can't bring to sight,
Won't by screws and levers be displayed.

– *Goethe, Faust Part One*

It is through science that we prove, but through intuition that we discover.

– *Henri Poincare*

When we walk through the world aesthetically, then we experience images like breath through the nostrils. Instead of the search for meanings, the perceptive sensitive response transforms events into images. This [is the] *via aesthetica.* ... aesthetics is the *via regia,* if we would restore our life in images and work out an appropriate method for the poetic basis of mind ...

– *James Hillman*

Thinking is more interesting than knowing, but not more than intuition.

– *Goethe*

My Land

The Land of Inner Activity

There is only one field of transformation. And no one is outside. This becomes clear when we think of the inner activity that takes place in us: the dimension of habits, attitudes, fears, dreams, perceptions, commitments, intentions. Such are the invisible aspects of human inner life that hinder and distort, or enable and support creative, connective actions in the 'outer' world. So, inner activity is as much a part of our own individual lives as the field of our visible actions and their consequences.

And yet, despite its centrality to both our own lives and our actions, it is possible for the inner field to be completely overlooked. We learn to function in the light whilst psyche is hidden in the dark: to function without noticing the unseen inner occurrences. But if we do not till and work this inner field then traumas cause only pain, and suffering remains suffering.

Many teachers, philosophers, activists and artists have explored ways of waking us from such sleep. In Bertold Brecht's words through strategies of 'internal mobilisation': of 'disruption' and 'making strange' (Verfremdung). Joseph Beuys's call to 'make the secrets productive' and 'scratching on the imagination' value the inner movement caused by such disruptions and shifts. In Jung and the archetypal psychologists, movement in this field can be enhanced by 'active imagination' or 'dreaming on the dream'.

All these strategies provoke inner activity that draw us out of sleep, and open up a sense of where our true power lies: a sense that 'every human being is an artist'. This is the field of invisible materials. Of formative forces. Forces that have immense 'sculptural' power to shape a better world. Social sculptural power!

23 DEC 2007

The Land of Inner Activity

Agile, not stuck in the given.
– *Shelley Sacks*

[We need to go] through a process of alienation: the alienation that is necessary to all understanding. When something seems 'the most obvious thing in the world' it means that any attempt to understand the world has been given up.
– *Bertold Brecht*

Often it is necessary to clarify a vague content by giving it visible form. [...] The hands often know how to solve a riddle with which the intellect has wrestled in vain. By giving it form, one goes on dreaming the dream in greater detail in the waking state, and the initially incomprehensible, isolated event is integrated into the sphere of the total personality, even though it may remain at first unconscious to the subject.
– *C. G. Jung*

On quiet days there is more inner activity.
– *Paul Klee*

We do not literally see images and hear metaphors; we perform an operation of insight which is seeing-through or hearing-into. We see through our hearing and listen-into through our seeing.
– *James Hillman*

My Land

The Land of Imagination

We can enter the real world with imagination, or create an unreal world. Both depend on our ability to create inner images.

But there is a difference. The creation of the real world that happens in me is real because I live into and explore existing phenomena: inner phenomena and outer phenomena. But I can only encounter these phenomena and let them live in me if I do so without prejudices and preconceived intentions, if I stay close to their reality. And staying close is part of the *art* of imagination. It means I must also become conscious of what I bring to the perception, of what I want or do not want to see.

But imagination can also be used to look away. To not look in. To shape a world of images that help us flee. From the pain and the needs, from the creatures and the questions, from the battlefields of profit and the fields of compassion. Images that keep us from coming to our senses. And so we create a world of illusion: of parallel worlds that seduce us, convince us and sustain us.

From this we see our imagination has the freedom to create all kinds of worlds. But is there not a form of imagination that goes beyond what is and yet remains a reality? An imagination that is able to see the world as a weave of interconnected life forms and processes all striving to extend and unfold themselves? A giant sculpture that we humans with the power to create – in other words, the capacity to make mistakes – engage in shaping? A sculpture, whose designer is each and every one of us?

Imagination is our first real step on the road to transformation.

The Land of Imagination

The point is that you start with any image … Contemplate it and carefully observe how the image begins to unfold or to change. Don't try to make it into something, just do nothing but observe what its spontaneous changes are. Any mental image you contemplate in this way will sooner or later change through a spontaneous association that causes a slight alteration of the image. You must avoid impatient jumping from one subject to another. Hold fast to the image you have chosen and wait until it changes by itself. Note all these changes and eventually step into the image yourself. If it is a speaking figure then say what you have to say to that figure and listen to what he or she has to say.

– *Carl Gustav Jung*

I'm enough of an artist to draw freely upon my imagination. Imagination is more important than knowledge. Knowledge is limited. Imagination encircles the world. Logic will get you from A from Z: imagination will get you everywhere.

– *Einstein*

The basic disease from which our culture might be dying is our minimization of images and myths, as well as our faith in a positivist, rationalist, acepticised civilization.

– *Gilbert Durand*

An image is not what you see, but the way you see.

– *Edward Casey*

My Land

The Land of Hearing

Joseph Beuys once described hearing as one of our most important 'organs of perception'.

But this organ is not simply the physical ear.

We hear with an inner sense that encounters the invisible aspect of things. An inner hearing that is not a passive process. I have to be very active to hear and to receive. I have to *listen into*.

And this is only possible without judging. Listening without sympathy or antipathy: staying with the other and staying with oneself. When I listen in this way – it awakens a closeness and the other *happens* in me.

And when I 'hear' you, I let you sound in me. Even things that have no apparent physical sound, like a person or a place, can be heard in us. One could say that the poetic continent *takes place* in me.

The voices of those who suffer from our actions also become clearer: of the animals and the trees, of the air and of the bees ... the voices of the rivers, water, moon, of day and of the night. The unheard sounds and the unacknowledged voices.

In this state of hearing, of inner amplification, we might be able to respond: at least, to open up a conversation.

I ring the bell. I hear the bell. I am the bell.

I respond to the bell.

4 Jan 2008

The Land of Hearing

Let us leave theories there and return to here's hear.
 – *James Joyce*

An old singer, somewhere in the Ukraine or in Galicia was once asked: 'To whom are you singing?' To which the cantor replies: 'I always sing to a point.' Question: 'Why do you do that?' The singer: 'I do that until the point starts singing to me.' 'Do you do this all the time?' 'Yes, until all points are singing.'
 – *Chassidic story*

Immanuel Kant said that the human being could 'listen into' nature's secrets.

'If I were a physician, and if I were allowed to prescribe just one remedy for all the ills of the modern world, I would prescribe silence.'
 – *Søren Kierkegaard*

... suffering is a definite sound in the world. It is audible. You can see it too. Whoever makes a real effort to perceive [it], will see suffering as a source of regeneration ... a source of precious matter that is released into the world [...] an invisible-visible sacramental substance, to be sure. And those who realise this today are the trees rather than people. ... That is why I plant trees. ... [not] because trees are beautiful. No, I say, the trees today are much more intelligent than humans. When the wind passes through their crowns, the very substance that the suffering people have brought to the earth moves through the crowns of the trees as well.
 – *Joseph Beuys*

My Land

The Land of Connectedness

As a child I soon learn that I am separate, not of the same body as my mother or father, not of the same family as you, not from the same street or town. I learn that there are things 'out there' that I can bump into. My eyes tell me this. My hands tell me this. But in doing this, my eyes and hands also deceive me.

They do not tell me that the breath I breathe is the same air that moves in and out of you. They do not tell me that the vibration that enters me as sound is the same vibration that enters you. They do not tell me that the whole world is connected in one huge vibratory field, from the smallest particle to the hugest planet. They do not tell me how delicately balanced everything is in this immense interconnected cosmos; how my thoughts effect you, how my doubts and uncertainties cause disturbances in the invisible pools. I see only the things within my field of vision. Perhaps this is why it is so difficult to develop care at a distance, care for others who produce what we need on the other side of the planet; care for rivers poisoned by the chemicals that clean our bathrooms. Perhaps this is why we could not foresee that every human intervention into the given world would have an effect at some level in the interconnected fabric of the cosmos.

Now the earth and all its beings show us the effects of our actions. Pain and damage have become our teachers. But we also have the chance to develop eyes that see the not visible; organs of perception that see our interconnectedness. And with these new eyes, new ears, new organs of understanding, we begin to see that we have the freedom and the potential to respond differently. We have the ability-to-respond. This is the basis of real responsibility.

The Land of Connectedness

There is no such thing as a separate object, event, or experience, because no part of the world can exist apart from all others. Rather, everything that looks like a separate entity is actually dependent on, and therefore interwoven with, something else. Everything (object, event, idea, experience, whatever) is made up of other things. Whatever appears to be an isolated 'thing' is actually a combination of its constituent elements. These elements are the influences from the other things with which it is interwoven. And those elements, too, are made up of other combinations. The world is an endless web of combinations.

– *Thich Nhat Hahn*

All things share the same breath – the beast, the tree, the man ...

– *Chief Seattle in response to the US government, 1854*

We need to recognise the non-human voices in every design process ... and design human habitats in ecological relationship. ... We beings are participants in an emergent process.

[*extract from Council of All Beings seminar, Berkeley, 1998*]

An injury to one, is an injury to all!

[*Slogan in the South African Liberation struggle*]

There is a direction which is very beautiful, ... of the organism being less and less locked into itself ... into its body structure and its relatively inadequate sense organs, toward a state where the organism can go out and share itself with others. Poetry in language is of the greatest order of the sharing of the inner self with the outer, with the non-self. In a way, that's the whole value of poetry, in a way it's on the highest level of human bonding.

– *Gary Snyder*

My Land

The Land of Encountering the Other

What takes place when one meets another? When I encounter what is 'not-I' in both the human and other than human sphere? In such encountering I participate in the other, which is one of our most wonderful gifts.

Such participation also creates shared destiny, although our destiny always remains our own.

Perhaps this is why as children we long to hear the stories of our elders. Through this I begin to live the great journey that lies ahead. What we call 'knowledge' begins as a journey rich in images, on which we embark with open heart, mind, eyes.

The poetic continent has to do with this inner journey, in which the meeting with the other is the door to the unknown. My curiosity, my questions, my interest beckon me through this portal – of the 'not I' into the 'other' world.

In each encounter the boundaries of self are extended. The more I gift my attention to both the other-in-myself and the other-out-there, the richer my psyche and my whole life becomes. This is one of the mysteries of the poetic continent and that this continent is not other than the world.

The respect that comes from such encountering of other is also vital in shaping a viable future, whose coherence depends on the myriad individual destinies that interweave and shape the common destiny of the world.

W
S
E

The Land of Encountering the Other

There is 'the silence of the pure listener'... through which the message of the other becomes the 'he/she in us', the silence of deep interest. It is threatened by another silence – the silence of disinterest, which assumes that there is nothing I want or can receive through the communication of the other. [...] the greater the distance between two worlds, the more this silence of [deep interest] is a sign of love.
– *Ivan Illich*

To meet another with respect and openness requires us to develop a sense for the other. It means listening carefully to the language that this person speaks. What is the thought that lies within it?
– *Albert Soesman*

Sustainability without the 'I'-sense is non-sense.
– *Shelley Sacks*

The idea of human dignity is above all a question of communication and understanding. Where there is a lack of dignity, there is always a lack of understanding as well. Human dignity begins with conversation: for the speaker and for the listener. I bestow dignity by listening and I bestow dignity through what I give in speaking. I bestow dignity through a genuine interest in the views of others, and notice that my interest in others also increases their potential for self-expression. Through such interest I grant the other person a dignity that is constructive. If we see all human beings as one single being then we know our neighbour is experiencing something that is important for each of us, and for all human beings.
– *Wolfgang Zumdick*

My Land

The Land of Freedom

How free are we really? To what extent are we determined by the forces of the past, by our egoism, our longing for power, our ambition?

Or are we capable of breaking the shell of the past that so often encapsulates us? Of freeing ourselves from the trajectories of power and egoism that drive us in inappropriate directions? What strategies will liberate us from unconscious and destructive psychological forms and enable us to shape new forms for a viable world? And where do these non-egotistic impulses come from ... these forces which enable us to direct ourselves in a way which is not only self concerned?

In opening ourselves to the world we allow the world to disclose itself in us. This evokes our capacity to love and to embrace what we normally experience as other: other to conquer, other to be feared, other to be exploited.

Only through this kind of love which brings the world to life in us, are we no longer driven to possess and control it. The more we fall in love with the world, the less our need to 'use' it.

This is the poetic continent. A being in the world free of ownership and false desire. This is the secret of freedom.

Although freedom means having freedom to enable freedom, and creating the external forms to make this possible, we not only need such external forms, but perpetually also to be conscious of what we think and how we think, as well as of our intentions.

25 Jan 2008

The Land of Freedom

If we were completely determined by the conditions – by our personal history and by the social conditions in which we live – we would not be able to change anything. But the sphere of freedom lies in us. We can and must move beyond the conditions, which now destroy both the earth and ourselves.

– *Shelley Sacks*

So long as one acts one is free, not before and not after: because to act and to be free is one and the same thing.

– *Hannah Arendt*

Life is how we respond to whatever confronts us.

– *C. G. Jung*

Art = Capital!

– *Joseph Beuys*

Thought reveals itself in action. Actions form habits. Habits create character. Character shapes destiny. Let us acquire good habits!

– *Morito Sugunuma Sensei*

We need to see deeply into things, to see how we can change, how we can transform our situation. To transform our situation is also to transform our minds. To transform our minds is also to transform our situation, because the situation is mind, and mind is situation … Freedom is not given to us by anyone; we have to cultivate it ourselves.

– *Thich Nhat Hahn*

My Land

The Land of Integration

One can be a stranger anywhere, even in one's own land: a stranger to the neighbours, to the authorities, and to oneself. One can even be a 'foreigner' at home. Overcoming such estrangement begins with a dialogue with oneself: a dialogue that also brings one closer to the world. This can be awakened by shared questions, which unite us ... by exploring alone and together what I think I'm doing in the world.

'Integrate' in Latin means to restore, reunite and to create higher wholes: new realities that are more than the sum of the parts. 'Individuation' on the level of the individual, is, from a Jungian perspective, the process of different aspects of a person re-constellating and reforming to become a coherent self. What would its parallel on a social level be? Is social integration conceivable that is more than the sum of the parts?

Since our notion of wholeness informs our methods of 'integration' we need to be conscious of the way in which any social wholeness is understood. What is the nature of the integration we strive for in our countries, cities and towns?

Enabling the emergence of a wholeness that is more than the sum of the parts is different from incorporating marginalised groups into the dominant world; from notions of 'inclusion' whose assumed normality leads to a flattening of richness and difference. If social integration like 'individuation' means the emergence of new and higher wholes, it needs openness to allow something new to emerge, as well as being prepared to risk that some things might have to be lost in the process of something much greater being gained. Although individual and social integration cannot be designed and created, we need to create arenas for social-imaginal work that are not simply a passive 'melting pot'!

E
S

The Land of Integration

There are different forms of dispossession, many, many ways in which people are deprived or subjected to all kinds of victimization – it doesn't have to be colonization. Once you allow yourself to identify with the people in a story, then you might begin to see yourself in that story even if on the surface it's far removed from your situation.
– *Chinua Achebe*

I believe that humanity has never accepted defeat against its enemies and will be victorious in the end. And war, hate, oppression and prejudice shall one day be replaced by what Hafiz, the great Persian poet, proclaimed love to be: the ultimate and immaculate basis of human relationships.
– *Faiz Ahmed Faiz*

As William Blake said of innocence and our initial oneness with the world, one could say too of integration – that we have to move from innocence to experience in order to come to a higher, more conscious form of innocence. This is a journey from our beginnings as one, through the fall into separateness and otherness, towards (re)integration.
– *Shelley Sacks*

Developing respect for diversity may be more effective when focused on the deep commonalities of universal human experience rather than the differences that exist between us.
– *Mind-Life Institute*

Integration (from Latin integrare, restore) is the merging of parts and the formation of higher-level wholes.

My Land

The Land of Globalisation

We need to share the resources and gifts of the world equitably – the physical ones, the ones of the psyche and the gifts of the mind. Only then will a truly social, global community be possible.

And the more every human being is able to flourish, the greater the wealth of this society will be.

But we are not here alone. The world is filled with other beings. And the earth is one of them ... with its own right to survive and to thrive. To perceive this wholeness, we need a different kind of thinking: a 'seeing' thinking, a 'listening' thinking, a thinking that enters, embraces and inhabits; that experiences the interconnections that are waiting to be perceived.

Then we will be able to create a global system that is viable for all, including the earth. The time for disconnected thinking is over. The time for integrative, seeing thinking is here! Such seeing thinking – which derives essentially from our imaginal capacity – promotes inner resilience and connective ideas.

We all make internal images when we dream and when we perceive. So every person has the capacity for imaginal thought. Every farmer, every teacher. Every gardener and factory worker. This capacity to 'see' internally, whether awake or in dreams, is the same capacity needed to discover and form new images of a non-exploitative, coherent world!

On this level we are already all artists – even if the significance of such capacities has been unclear. In them lies our transformative power to see the problems and the possibilities that lay the basis for the 'permanent conference' and the shaping of a viable world.

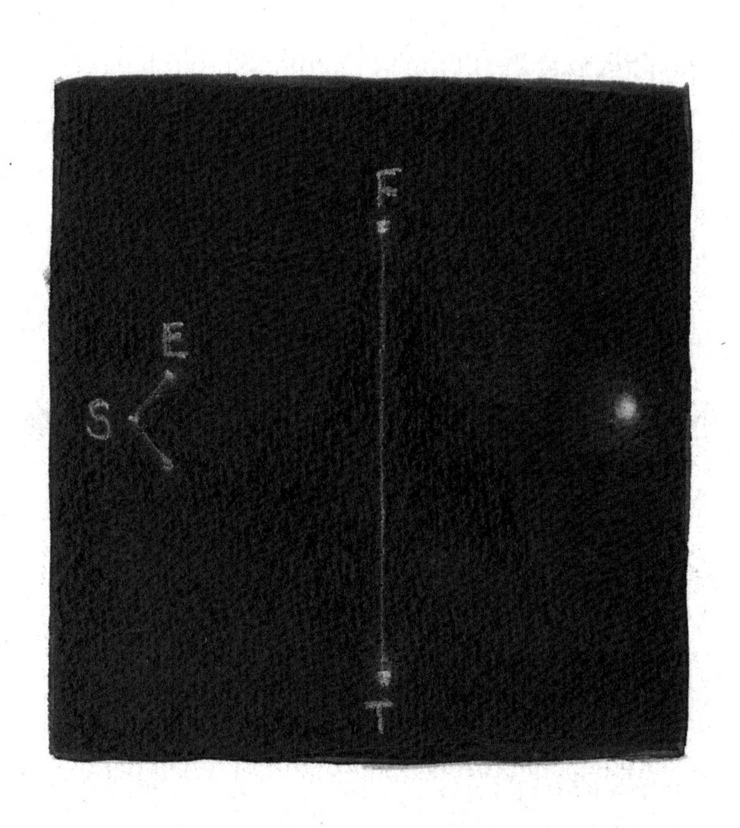
F
E
S
T

The Land of Globalization

A community of cooperating humans is all the more healthy, the less the individual person claims the proceeds of his performance for himself. In other words, the more of these proceeds he gives to his co-workers, the more his own needs get satisfied, not from his own performance, but from that of the others.

– *Rudolf Steiner*

The possibility for all people on the planet to communicate with each other arises to the extent that an awareness of [planetary] unity stirs ... and such thoughts derive their power from the fact that they are relevant for every human being.

– *Karl Jaspers*

The world is the world of taking-place. It is the place where there is room/place for everyone. The world is nowhere. It is the opening up of the dimension of a possibility to co-exist.

– *Jean-Luc Nancy*

Awareness of interdependence makes it immediately evident that each of us shares responsibility for all that happens and will happen: there is no phenomenon in the universe that does not immediately concern us. As soon as we recognize that responsibility, we are moved to act to improve the situation: if we are very aware, we can do something to change the course of things ... and this means changing both situation and self.

– *Thich Nhat Hahn*

We need to uncover and experience our innate connections with each other and with the systemic, healing powers of the web of life, so that [we] may be enlivened and motivated to play our part in creating a sustainable civilization.

– *Joanna Macy*

My Land

The Land of Determination

'Yes we can' and 'another world is possible' are two phrases that reflect the spirit of the times and the feelings of a great number of people across the planet, as almost no other. They embody a confidence that it is possible to overcome warmongering attitudes, racism, chauvinism and injustices like inequality, poverty, dependence and lack of education – and ensure a dignified life for every person on earth.

Despite all the widespread threats and crises, we are nevertheless closer to this 'other world' than ever before. There is a growing awareness of the planet and of humanity as one interrelated being, in which everyone shares responsibility for the existence of every other.

But being determined and committed to this is clearly not enough. How many reformations and revolutions aim to create, if not a good world, at least something better. But this has often not been the case – sometimes even the best will and intentions have ended in disaster.

And so, if I am determined I must also be able to see and evaluate what I am determined about and where the source of this determination lies. I need to have an image of the consequences of such determination, both for and beyond myself. Although I can and must talk this through with others, ultimately I need to explore, understand and take responsibility for the consequences of such determination and intentions myself.

If our determination is rooted in a love of the world and a genuine humanity, if it is inspired by true liberty, equality and solidarity, it will also be the source of an egalitarian culture concerned not only with human wellbeing, but the health and right to life of all other beings as well.

The Land of Determination

We can't allow ourselves to go under!
 – *Beuys*

Another world is possible!
 – *World Social Forum*

... escape from necessity? Like children? But then one would lose the value of life.
 – *Simone Weil*

Compassion is not reaching out to an 'other'. It is (as the literal meaning of the word suggests) 'feeling together with'. Compassion means experiencing one's own fate and the fate of the supposed other as identical. Therefore, it means experiencing the other's suffering as one's own suffering.
 – *Thich Nhat Hahn*

Read no more – look!
Look no more – go!
 – *Paul Celan*

Situations change, opportunities appear. If missed they do not come again.
 – *Karl Jaspers*

Almost everyone has loved the world, if given two handfuls of earth.
 – *Bertolt Brecht*

My Land

The Land of Citizenship

In German the term for citizenship, 'Burgerschaft', although having the same root as 'burgerlich' or bourgeois – does not necessarily mean the sweet life for myself that excludes the other. Citizenship or 'Burgerschaft' is a radical proposition. It is what we can achieve [schaffen] together.

However, although our notion of citizenship has evolved greatly over the centuries, and we have got clearer about our rights – usually confirmed as laws – the state of the world makes clear that we have not yet focused enough on the responsibilities and relationships of citizens to each other, or within the vast matrix of other beings with whom we share this world. In the shared physical territory of 'the city', 'the land', 'the planet', we have to shape another territory: a poetic domain of exchange and listening, of empathy, of thinking together and living together, in which the social imagination lives and moves.

We have to shape *a social sculpture* consisting of forms and processes in which the individual is not denied and overshadowed by the needs of the whole, and the whole is not forgotten in the attempt to fulfil my needs at the expense of yours. To shape the social sculpture I have to be an active citizen, who listens, perceives, imagines, speaks and acts; as passionate about the whole as I am about my own needs, and in constant dialogue with others and with the world. This kind of relatedness is the path to ecological citizenship and the global cultural commons!

Joseph Beuys called the creative social space for the negotiation and transformation of our thinking 'the permanent conference'. The meeting and active engagement with each other in this autonomous zone is where transformative action begins – and might fulfil what Hannah Arendt intended in her expanded notion of 'action'.

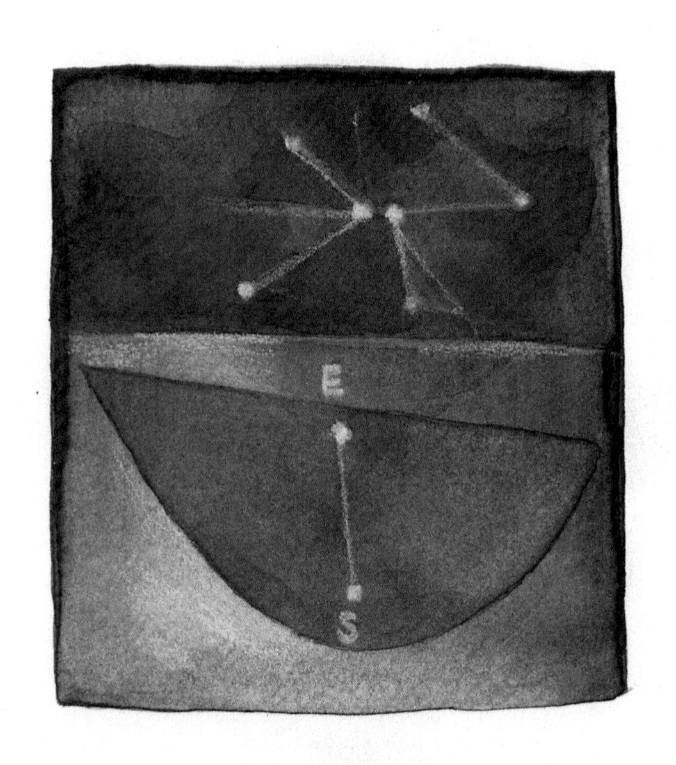
E
S

The Land of Citizenship

Since the individual and society 'inter-are,' each must nourish the other, or both will wither. The preservation of oneself is the same thing as the preservation of all; the improvement of oneself is the same thing as the improvement of all; the healing of one's own suffering is the same thing as the healing of all suffering. This is compassion.
– *Thich Nhat Hahn*

Compassion and empathy are fundamental to the development of… a kinder, more just, and more caring society. As emotions that embody an awareness of one's interconnection with others, they serve as a foundation for altruism, cooperation, helping, and other social behavior. … human beings have a natural propensity for compassion and empathy but need specialized training to extend this feeling beyond the immediate circle of family, friends, and others we identify with closely. A key challenge in educating world citizens is expanding this circle of concern to encompass the wider, interdependent world in all its diversity.
– *The Dalai Lama*

I must know that all that wealth does not belong to me; what belongs to me is the right to a honourable livelihood, no better than that enjoyed by millions of others. The rest of my wealth belongs to the community and must be used for the welfare of the community.
– *Gandhi*

In 1987 the UN coined the phrase 'think globally, act locally'. For the citizen, thinking globally means to recognise that our actions and way of life have consequences that go beyond our own local environment; acting locally means to assume our share of responsibility by locally changing our way of life in order to act for sustainable development at the global level. … sustainable development is not only a matter of concern for international decision makers, it is also every citizen's responsibility.
– *Council of Europe – Education for Democratic Citizenship and Human Rights*

My Land

The Land of Love

Can we meet anything, a tree, a creature, a situation, another, if we do not first meet ourselves and respect what we meet?

The unconditional love of parents for their child, like the cosmos for all its beings, is the powerful force that supports us through our lives. Like the life force that flows through the plant, I am carried by my love: my first love the gift of life, my second love – the mysteries of manifestation – that I encounter in and beyond us.

But what love do I need to stand courageous and strong?

Oh beautiful world
From the temple of our shelter I peer out
Refusing the sense of helplessness
Determined to overcome despair
About the damage that we have done.

Oh beautiful earth
From the temple of our shelter I step out
With two open hands, two feet
Ready to transform and repair
Carrying my gift of loving into your continents and lands.

I come in the name of love
I bring the gifts received in birth
The imagination, the creative potential
It is all for you, dear world.

With such love we can embrace what is thriving and sound
We can work on what has been spoiled
We can re-envision and shape a more coherent world.

24 Jan 2008

The Land of Love

What actually drives me to act? In the space between volition and thought, the heart acts, and love … is the only motive.
– *Joseph Beuys*

I love you tomato because you taste of tomato
And I know your wetness
It is for my mouth, but first for your propagation

I love you apple because your pale golden flesh
Takes me into your world; awakens desire in me,
Like the Eros in your seeds, waiting to meet the soil

I love you carrot, so vast, yet uncomplicated
Your radiating orange and green
That never doubts what you are, returns me to myself

You give me truth, as I taste you,
when I hold you, when I smell you

As you do, loved one in the boat,
in the world, in the stars
the one I am waiting to join

Although time is written into our skin
The future is woven into our heart
– *Shelley Sacks*

Yes, our task is to take this provisional, perishable earth so deeply, so patiently, and passionately into ourselves that its being 'invisibly' resurrects in us.
– *Rainer Maria Rilke*

My Land

The Land of Answers

Like scents in the evening garden, I follow the questions and come to the flower, often hidden from view. In the half-light, at the edges of the everyday, in both the wonder and the suffering, the answers lie waiting.

If I make a quiet space, I can hear them in myself, in the other, and in the forms of the cosmos that are visible all around. The human being is one of these forms.

In this space where I can widen my view, it is possible to see that the human being is a freedom-being, able to develop a world of consciousness and care; to see a world of interconnectedness that aches for the humans to become aware: to develop new organs of perception, new ways of living, and a new form of social and ecological love.

As my questions activate the thought-field, faint echos begin to sound.

In this sense the questions are trajectories that mobilise us internally, that move us to participate in the process of unfolding answers.

Antwort (Zuversicht)

The Land of Answers

Einstein was once asked: What is the most important question that one can ask? His answer: 'Is the universe a friendly place, or not?'

My life is my message ...
– *Gandhi*

There is a process of 're-storying' peoples who had been knocked silent by all kinds of dispossession. ... this 're-storying' will continue and will eventually result in a balance of stories among the world's peoples. [...] the universal civilization I dream about ... is something that we will create. All those who are saying it is there are suggesting that it's there by default – they are saying to us, let's stop at this point and call what we have a universal civilization. [But] if we want a universal civilization, we should work to bring it about. And when it appears, [...] we will know, because it will be different from anything we have now. [...] We have to hold this conversation, which is a conversation of stories, a conversation of languages, and see what happens.
– *Chinua Achebe*

... but *what* is a rabbit?
– *Rosa van Wyk*

'Tell me Rabbi, what is the secret of the ritual bath?' 'If you ask in this way, perhaps you've found your own answer, and just want to know if I approve of it. So, what do you think?' 'Since you want to know, Rabbi, I will tell you what I think, but it is not an answer. I just think: you go down, and even further down, and when you are all the way down, then you really bend down, that's all I know.'
– *Martin Buber*

My Land

The Land of Joy

We now know that birds sing not only for all sorts of functional reasons, including the continuity of the species, but also because they love to sing. Singing is their work and their pleasure.

The personal and social world is our workplace. But in dividing work and play, pleasure and leisure, human beings are alienated from the joy inherent in working to shape a viable world and the unfolding of our full capacities.

Joy is like the force that rises in the spring. Joy flows through what we do when our creativity confronts necessity. Joy is the honey that flows in our lives when we are able to realise our abilities.

'Marx describes how by selling her/his own bodily powers, a worker's well-being and identity are impoverished by removal from his or her own self-directed capacity to work creatively.' [Ariel Salleh]

This is why we need an unconditional basic income, not wages for labour ... so that joy is part of our daily work. We need an income that entitles and does not oblige; a means of surviving that is not dependent on the work we do.

We will also need to find ways to share the less pleasant work as well as the inspiring work.

So that everyone has the possibility to allow the potential in themselves to unfold freely: to allow their own song to be sung.

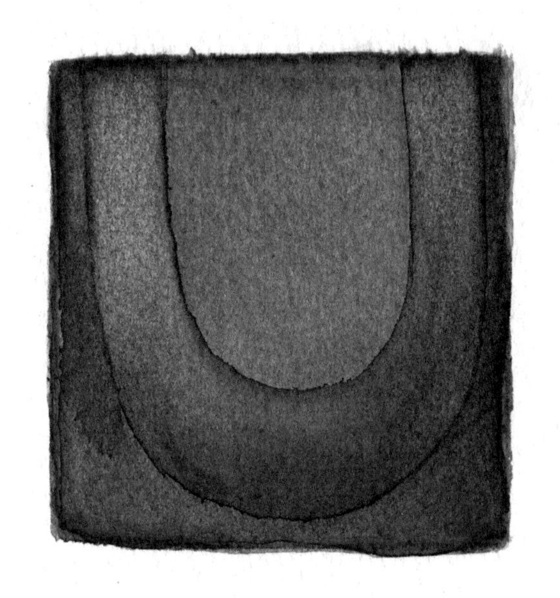

25 Jan 2008

The Land of Joy

Income is a human right! A human right. It is quite simple! And income cannot be derived from work that is embodied in a product. The part that a human being plays [in the production] of the liver-sausage cannot be determined.

– *Beuys*

Epiphany

this is the place of eros
of desire   to understand

the place of homo economicus
of taking in   and giving out

of the global struggle for freedom
sustained   by ancient joy

– *Shelley Sacks*

A stream of air moves through us, as if we are being breathed by life. Everyone in this city, on this planet, is being filled with this life, right at this moment. We are all sustained in a vast living web.

– *Council of All Beings*

This delicate little Aeolian harp that nature has set at the entrance to our breathing is really a sixth sense, which followed and surpassed the others. It quivers at the merest movement of metaphor; it permits human thought to sing.

– *Gaston Bachelard*

He who binds himself to a joy
Does the winged life destroy
He who kisses the joy as it flies
Lives in eternity's sun rise

– *William Blake*

My Land

The Land of Thankfulness

We must guard against *thanking* becoming routine. Thanking needs to be thought, to be a conscious process.

Which means being aware that we always have others to thank for our existence; without other people we would not exist. This is a good antidote for arrogance.

Our life is a fabric, worked by many hands.

All cultures have different forms of giving thanks. But these forms are increasingly lost as the forces of contemporary culture deprive us of this intuition.

And so it is ever more important that our unconscious attitude to giving thanks changes to one of thoughtfulness in the thanking.

Darkens

Land of Thankfulness

Thinking and thanking, in our language, are words of one and the same origin.
 – *Paul Celan*

Ecologically considered, it is not primarily our verbal statements that are 'true' or 'false', but rather the kind of relations that we sustain with the rest of nature. A human community that lives in a mutually beneficial relation with the surrounding earth is a community, we might say, that lives in truth, [...] A civilization that relentlessly destroys the living land that it inhabits is not well acquainted with truth, regardless of how many supposed facts it has amassed regarding the calculable properties of its world.
 – *David Abram*

Dome

I hear the song
Of birds
In the morning
Half awake
Their voices
One voice
One voice
One song
– *Wolfgang Zumdick*

There is a river that runs from thanks to truth,
through 'applaud' to plausible,
and from celebrating to being true to what is!
 – *Shelley Sacks*

My Land

The Land of Forgiveness

There is conscious action and unconscious action: action that is freely chosen and action that I do without thinking and choosing; actions shaped by days and years of habits; ways of being, thinking and reacting that I am taught and that I inherit from my personal world and the wider world into which I am born.

When I reflect on these actions – I see that some are more humane, more valuable, more creative than others.

In this moment – as I notice the actions and deeds that are not in tune with what I need, others need, the earth needs, with the world of other beings, I can be harsh with myself and condemn my actions. Or I can forgive. Forgive myself because I was blinded by habit, or because it is sometimes so difficult for the action to match the intention.

This is the best possible of all worlds because it is the field of 'working on what has been spoilt'; the world where becoming conscious includes forgiving oneself, forgiving the other and doing it better in the next freely given moment.

This is the realm of forgiveness, in which to cultivate forgiveness: the realm where responsibility is not strengthened by shame and condemnation. This is the realm where responsibility – my ability to respond in a more connected way – is increased when I shine the light of mind on my mistakes and explore them as bitter fruits for nourishing better deeds. In forgiving myself I am able to forgive you, and to taste the fruits of this parallel world of milk and honey.

13 Jan 2008

The Land of Forgiveness

if i open myself to my mistakes
i will not turn into stone

let us not turn back, only forward
into our buried thoughts
and our wounds, with love

in this way we will return
to the continent of rushing rivers
of atmospheres, of earth
to the poetic continent

that still gifts us the forgiveness to go on.
– *Shelley Sacks*

Glorious morning
Gift me your light
Gift me your breath
Spread your coral
Over my pityful mind
Over my complaining, faint heart
In joy
Let me rise

Glorious morning
Refresh me with
Your berries
Lay them
On my dry lips
Give honey
And fresh juices
To my dried out husk
– *Wolfgang Zumdick*

My Land

The Land of Death

Suppose we could take a look at this world from the other side, from beyond this life. Who would we encounter? And what would confront us? From this vantage point, how would our life on earth now seem? What would it reflect, what would it conceal? And ... doesn't art enable such an altered perspective? Isn't everything that arises in the artistic mode, always to some extent dependent on being able to see life from the perspective of death?

Clearly there are two deaths: the one that we experience in life, and the other that marks the threshold to another state of being. The phrase 'die into becoming' reminds one of both our mortality and our task: of our deeper connection to existence.

Death is always a bridge and a transition: a turning point after which a transformation is needed. Physical death is something we cannot avoid. Even with the most developed forms of medicine. But this other 'small' death, the one that we experience over and over again in life, this we can overcome. This we can confront. But we can only do this as long as we face that which brings this death. By so doing we realise that something living can emerge from this.

Perhaps it is this that we then encounter in our 'big' death, enabling us to face it with less fear, provided we have faced these 'small' deaths during life.

1 feb 2008

The Land of Death

Our being is a being-towards-death.
– *Heidegger*

... I have survived everything, and I will also survive death. Heidegger maintains that man is a being made for death; all poets, however, create resurrection, intone a triumphant hurrah in the face of death.
– *José Lezama Lima*

Question to Joseph Beuys

ACHILLE BONITO OLIVA: [...] if man is a god, why does he face the question of death? How does he deal with it?

BEUYS: Because he accepts death as the methodology of creation. Because he needs it. Because he has a fundamental understanding that without death he would not be able to live consciously. If he was only concerned with life, he might as well be a piece of seaweed. He is however also concerned with death, and therefore with spirit, with form. If I hit my head against a hard edge, I wake up. In other words, death keeps me awake.

If death was only negative, then dying would be an unimaginable action.
– *Emil Mihaj Cioran*

Let him be just and deal kindly with my people, for the dead are not powerless. Dead, did I say? There is no death, only a change of worlds.
– *Chief Seattle*

My Land

Pathways on the Poetic Continent

The poetic continent is not so much about changing things and external transformation as it is about a transformation of perspective and attitude. And yet it has everything to do with changing things and with transformation in the world.

This apparent contradiction, overcome only when we understand the connection between inner and outer work, is what normally divides those who believe in transformation into two camps: those concerned with work in the inner field and those engaged in outer work in the world.

The 'lands' you have entered with us through this book open up pathways that connect inner and outer work. But there are many more lands. There is in fact a land for every human capacity, feeling, attitude, quality that needs to be developed in us and brought onto the physical continents of this planet. In this sense the 'lands' in this book could be almost infinitely extended. This is one of the reasons that this book is also a 'workbook' for each reader. As you travel through our and others contributions to this journey toward a re-latedness, we hope that you will use the spaces to discover and map these as yet undisclosed lands of your own, as an ecological citizen.

Being an ecological citizen can be understood to mean being connected to the world in such a way that one realises where action is needed. But it makes no sense to put oneself under moral pressure. We need to experience the necessity for any change in our self. And this has to do with the lived understanding and longing for coherence, which is also a longing for order, for beauty.

Developing a sense for and redefining beauty and the poetic in this way takes us into an engaged state – beyond working out solutions to problems – in which our entire being longs for things to be sound, to be coherent. It also means developing the capacities to see what needs to be done from this perspective of beauty as coherence and interconnectedness.

Our sense of beauty – not often understood in this way – is what really gives us a sense of the disturbed interconnections. When something like Fukushima occurs it is not only a technical disaster that requires incredibly creative technical solutions and responses, but it is also an aesthetic disaster: a destruction of beauty… beauty as understood by mathematicians and scientists like Einstein, and by ecological thinkers and activists who experience the disturbance of the poised interrelationships as a destruction of the beautiful and the good.

And now to turn for a moment to Schiller's idea and call for the 'aesthetic education of the human being' and an 'aesthetic state'. This is not to invoke the past for its own sake, but to bring it into our work in the present for a different kind of future. The 'aesthetic state' envisaged by Schiller is not to do with a separated world of art, or ideas of beauty disconnected from daily life, but rather with the kind of connective coherence that a humane and ecologically viable future requires.

Oh beautiful world. Oh poetic continent. Where the human beings could become so attuned, attentive and enlivened that they develop ways of living that do not unnecessarily negate or destroy, but enhance our capacities to experience the beautiful and the disturbance of the beautiful, as well as ways of establishing the beautiful in the world.

Pathways on the Poetic Continent

like leaves in august

deep green, enlightened by light
light breathed into the blue

drawn through cloud
bowed toward earth

architects of tree, light woven
player and played

skydancer
thought in hands

countenance of radiance embodied and seen

tree

your crown a mountain
of green coral
and the gulf stream of summer
dances its winds
in vigorous sweeps

fish shoals drifting, clouds
through
wind and branches.
– *Wolfgang Zumdick*

although the moon was held in the lime tree
the children longed for music
that could not be shared
until a better world was shaped
from the givens and the mess
until they all began to work on what had been spoiled
he said this was the new placenta, created together
no longer given from above
– *Shelley Sacks*

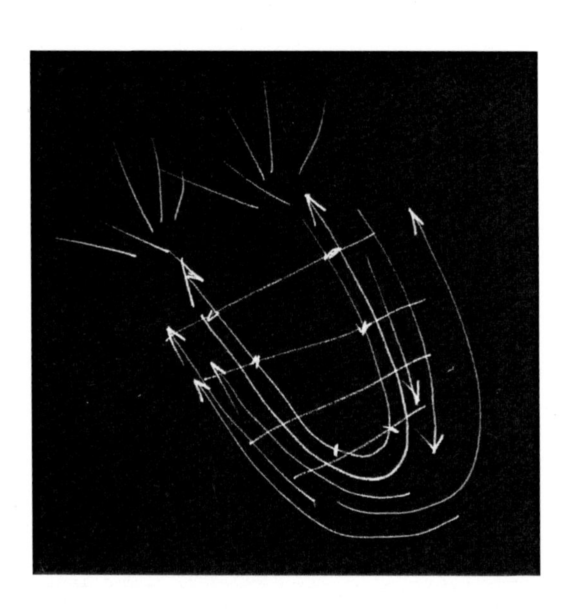